D0297786

Meg's Story

MEG'S STORY

Get Real!

Straight Talk About Drugs

By Gilda Berger

Photographs by Barbara Kirk

The Millbrook Press Brookfield, Connecticut

Please note: the people shown in the photographs in
this book are models and are not in any way related to
the real people depicted in the text.

Library of Congress Cataloging-in-Publication Data

Berger, Gilda.

Meg's story : get real! : straight talk about drugs /
by Gilda Berger ; photographs by Barbara Kirk.
p.   cm.
Summary: A young girl describes how she became addicted to drugs,
her experiences as an addict, and her struggles to recover and take
charge of her life.
ISBN 1-56294-102-X (lib. bdg.)
1. Teenagers—United States—Drug use—Case studies—Juvenile
literature.   2. Narcotic addicts—Rehabilitation—United States—
Case studies—Juvenile literature.   1. Drug abuse.   2. Narcotic
addicts—Rehabilitation.   I. Kirk, Barbara, ill.   II. Title.
HV5824.Y68B473   1992
362.29'0835—dc20   91-21515   CIP   AC

! Preface

What causes a person to become a drug addict?

In the past, it was thought that only people on the fringes of society became addicted to drugs. Many experts also believed that addiction was caused by a single factor, such as heredity, a troubled family life, or problems with peers.

Now we know that addiction is a far more complicated affair. Addicts are found in all segments of society—young and old, rich and poor, black and white—and throughout the entire United States. Experts now agree that many different factors can trigger a problem with drugs and keep it going.

Meg's Story is an actual, first-person account of a young person's involvement with drugs. Far from a typical addict, Meg is solidly middle-class, bright and talented, a good student, frank, outgoing, cheerful, and has many friends and a supportive family. And far from the more usual ways of getting started on drugs, Meg's addiction began after she suffered a serious head injury and was treated with a very strong prescription medicine.

At first, Meg's story of substance abuse may seem different from others that you may have heard. But her problems and concerns are not. They are shared by all addicts—whatever their background or cause of addiction.

For our interview, Meg arrived at my home at precisely the time we had set. She was tall, blond, and blue-eyed. She walked through the door and into the living room with great confidence. Very politely she refused my offer of a soda, saying that she would prefer water. "I don't trust myself with soda," she said.

For the next few hours Meg told her story while I kept the tape recorder going. Even when tears came to her eyes as she recalled especially painful incidents, she insisted on continuing and on being completely frank and honest.

At times, listening to Meg and meeting her steady gaze, I found it hard to imagine her stealing thousands of dollars to support her habit and being arrested for dealing cocaine. In many ways, it was easier to picture her in her present circumstances—enjoying her family and friends, going to college, and working.

Gradually, though, her words began to sink in. I began to realize the serious nature of her problem. Meg still craves drugs. But she is struggling to overcome her addiction and is far along in her recovery.

Meg's story shows how anyone can become addicted. It also points up something else: Every addict can get help and move toward recovery.

Gilda Berger
April 1991

Meg's Story

I guess you could say that I grew up in a middle-class home. My father is an accountant, and he's always had his own business. We lived in a nice house with enough money for everything we needed. You know, Mom and Dad always bought us nice clothes. We got a new car every couple of years. And we went on lots of vacations. Stuff like that.

Mine was what you'd call a "good family." I have a sister, Ellen, who is just about a year older than me. So in those days that made me the baby.

When we were little kids, my sister and I were so close in age that the quarreling was incredible. We fought and fought and fought. But underneath it we really loved each other. It sounds crazy, I know. We were very close—but we fought all the time.

When I did something wrong as a kid, it was always, "Let's sit down and talk." When I did something *really* wrong my parents might give me the wooden spoon across my bottom, just like everyone else. But they were not usually very rough.

As a kid, I was always physically very strong. I guess you'd call me a tomboy. So I got into a lot of fights. I didn't go out looking for them, but I guess I developed the attitude of being athletic and tough. I wanted to have that reputation. I laugh about it now because I got into the most stupid kinds of fights.

I remember I got into a fight with this big kid in third grade. He picked up my shirt one time. Really there was nothing to see. But I gave him two black eyes, and he had bruises from one end of his body to the other. Now it's something I just look back on and laugh about. But that was basically my personality.

When I was a younger kid, I felt good about myself. I think I had a pretty carefree life. In grade school I was always a straight-A student. And I was always getting prizes for sports. I had one big dream. It was to go to the Olympics as a gymnast or horseback rider. Those were my two big strengths.

Young Meg biking with friends.

I had two good friends in school, Amy and Jenny. We did everything together. Gymnastics and riding. After school, we'd go over to each other's house and tumble and do back flips. Saturdays we'd go to the horse ranch where we'd ride the ponies. Everyone always said I was the best.

But one day it all changed. Something happened that I'll never get over. My whole world fell in. It was the sort of thing that could have happened to anyone. But it happened to me.

It was the day before Thanksgiving. Eight years ago. I had just turned twelve years old.

That morning, I was out riding bicycles with my sister, Ellen, and Amy, my best friend at the time. I made a turn on my bicycle to go back home. But I didn't see this car coming around the corner. As I turned, the car slammed into me.

I don't remember any of the accident. You know, your brain sort of blocks it out. But I was taken to the hospital. I still don't even know how long I was there. It's something my family and I never really talk about.

Anyway, the doctors told my parents that I had three cracks in my skull—*three* skull fractures. They didn't think I was going to make it. If I did, they said I was going to be a vegetable or something.

I was in a coma for a couple of days. The

first thing I remember is getting out of bed to go to the bathroom. I looked in the mirror and saw my face was all cut up. And my hair was, like, teased out to here with blood. I thought to myself, "Oh, my God!"

My dad ran over. He and I are real close. He was in tears. I didn't know how to handle it. So I broke down and started to cry, too.

The doctors prescribed phenobarbital, a barbiturate, for me. Then they let me go home. Now that I know a little more about it, I would think that phenobarbital was very strong medicine to give to a twelve-year-old, especially one who had never been exposed to anything stronger than aspirin. The phenobarbital was supposed to prevent the convulsions that can come after a bad head injury. But it also gave me my first real taste of drugs. I don't know. Maybe that's what started it all for me. I'm not sure.

Anyway, after the hospital, I stayed at home for a while. I was very depressed because I couldn't do anything. My balance was way off. I couldn't tumble or do trampoline work. I wanted to do my sports—like soccer and softball. But, of course, I couldn't because of what had happened to me.

Also, because of what had happened to my head I became a different person. I went quickly from being a pretty nice kid to being a very re-

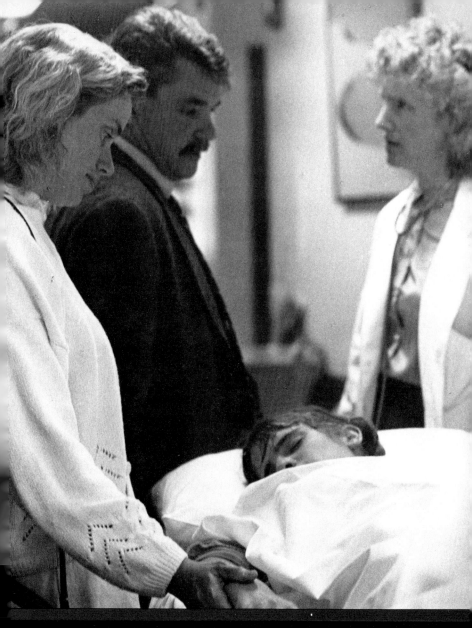

Meg's parents talk to the doctor about Meg's condition.

bellious, hateful person. I hated just for the sake of hating. I guess I always was very strong-willed and bullheaded to a point, but not really rebellious.

We had a hard time at home. My parents were devastated. The whole family practically just fell apart at that point. I was acting very violent with my family. Very violent and very aggressive.

When I eventually went back to school, kids kept asking if they could do something for me. They treated me like a cripple or something because I was acting so strange. But I always said, "No, I can do it myself." I was *very* independent. So I sort of threw my anger at them, in a way. I separated myself from my friends.

At the same time I started taking more and more of the phenobarbital. The pheno calmed me down quite a bit. And I was told to be very careful not to get angry or anything like that.

I thought the drug was also helping with the terrible headaches I got after the accident. I didn't mention these to anyone, except maybe to a couple of friends. But I wouldn't tell my parents because they would have made me go to the doctor. I hated doctors. I didn't want them near me. I was afraid they might stop me from doing things or, even worse, put me back in the hospital.

I never knew that you couldn't drink and

take phenobarbital at the same time. I never thought of alcohol as a drug—which it is. Anyway, I took my first beer at a New Year's Eve party. I was still on the phenobarbital. I passed out, right in the middle of the party.

After that, my parents spoke with the doctors. They took me off the pheno. But that didn't really help.

When I was studying, that's when I had the most trouble. I couldn't focus or concentrate for very long. I had to do a lot of reading for social studies, which became one of the harder courses for me. When I would read the page, the words would sometimes just blur out.

It was very frustrating for me. I couldn't study for big chunks of time because I would get severe headaches. I'd deal with the headaches by taking aspirin—two, three, or four at a time. Sometimes they would do good and sometimes they wouldn't. It just depended.

The headaches were always there, more or less. But then I started getting used to them. It was sort of like a tight shoe. It was just something you lived with. Even to this day, I have headaches. Not as bad as they were before, but definitely there.

So anyway, one thing led to another. And pretty soon I started hanging out with a different crowd. I guess you'd call them the wrong crowd.

They were mostly high school kids and kids out of school.

I think a lot of the problem had to do with growing up in this town. It has to do with the money that's around. Most of the kids are very materialistic. My cousin Suzy is a good example. She won't wear a shirt unless it's a Gap shirt or a Polo shirt—or at least a fifty-dollar shirt. Everything has to be graded by monetary value.

Another problem about growing up around here is that there's nothing for kids to do. We have one movie theater. But you can't go there every night. We have a bowling alley. But they don't let you hang out there, even though it's supposed to be open to the public. And they charge about three dollars to bowl a game. That's outrageous!

So you end up hanging out in town. We used to hang out behind the grade school. We'd go there and, you know, drink and smoke pot.

As I said, my best friend before the accident was Amy. She was the kind of kid who did her school work and her sports and never got into trouble. You know, Amy was riding with us when I got hit. But after that she really didn't know how to approach me. It's understandable. I don't know how I would feel if she had gotten hit. You know—how do you talk to someone who's supposed to be dead?

Meg hangs out in town with her new friends.

So after the accident, I made two new friends, Jane and Linda. I don't know how we got to be best friends. I'd never really spoken to either of them in grade school. But for some reason I felt very close to these girls. Jane and Linda weren't bad kids. But the three of us together were just bad news.

When I was with them, I felt that I was better than the kids I used to know. I was more mature. I handled more things. Also, I think the new crowd offered me more of a release. Most of the new group didn't even know I had been in an accident. They were all older kids. Cool kids.

That's how it was that summer. Pretty crazy. I was one of the few kids from Sandy Neck hanging out in town. The kids in Sandy Neck and the kids in town—they never got along. The "townies" always wore the jeans and the jean jackets and the tee shirts. They didn't bathe all the time. Some of them were very unclean.

Also, with the kids I used to know, everything was so serious. With the new kids, you know, we'd all get high and laugh and joke. Sometimes I would get high just to pass out—just to stop the headaches.

Then, in the September after the accident, I turned thirteen. I was definitely bad after that. I went from nice clothes to wearing my tight denim jeans and, well, tough clothes. My whole attitude then went from being rebellious to being just mean.

Now that I was into the drugs, I didn't just fight people who made me mad. I'd go out looking for fights. I was just horrible!

As I said, my sister and I always fought a lot. But that was nothing compared to how we were when I really started getting high, and she didn't exactly keep quiet about it. As soon as Ellen found out, she told my Mom everything. So, of course, we started fighting worse than ever.

My parents didn't really know how to handle my outrageous behavior. They didn't want to face the fact that I was smoking pot and probably doing other drugs. For a long time, they just refused to believe it. And when they finally did, they thought it was just a phase. They kept waiting for me to grow out of it.

I don't know how I would have handled me if I was them. For one thing, I was never home. I always came home late—you know, the typical scenario. I wouldn't come home after school. I'd hang out behind the school. And, even when they were trying to discipline me, I would never listen to them.

My father would scream at me and I'd scream at him. Then my father would give it to me. Like he'd say, "Who do you think you are?" But I don't think anything ever got through my thick

*Meg's father pulls her away from her friends
and tries to convince her to come home.*

head—it's hard wood. It got to the point where they knew I wouldn't come home.

So Mom and Dad would come after me. They would come around behind the school. And we would all be hanging out there, drinking beer and smoking pot. And they would come up holding a flashlight.

"Have you seen Meg?" they'd ask.

Then all my friends would split. They were scared to death of my parents.

I remember one time my father came walking toward us. We were all high. Somebody shouted, "Oh, my God! It's the cops!"

And they all split. But I knew it was my dad. So I just sat there. And, you know, he'd want to take me home. And I thought, "It's all right, he's my father." And I said, "I'm coming, okay. I know it's time to go home."

Now, I don't want to give you the impression that all this didn't bother me. I was used to Dad being mad at me at this point. But it still hurt when Dad came after me and yelled and gave me holy hell.

The worst time was once when I came home really, really wasted. A terrible thing happened. I got into an argument with Mom and for some reason I hit her. Right away my dad stepped in and he hit me right back. I think I deserved it. In fact, I think I probably deserved about ten more of them.

By the time the summer before high school rolled around, I'd made the changeover to the harder stuff. Not that there was pressure from anyone to try acid and stuff. It was just that I was hanging out with that type of crowd, you know, the jailbirds. Some of the people had just got out of jail or had been in jail before. They were all out of school. At least most of them were.

Also, most of them were older than me. I was only fourteen. But I looked older when I was fourteen than I do now, for some reason. So nobody knew how old I was.

Anyhow, that's when my using real heavy drugs came in. I mean, like taking acid and mescaline. Up until that time I was mostly just smoking pot and drinking beer.

I believe it was that summer that I also became sexually active. That was another big thing. I was very promiscuous after that.

A lot of times, it wasn't that I felt I had to sleep with the guys that gave me drugs. That's not the way it was. But I was very naive about relationships. I didn't see that these guys were just using me. It was always, like, maybe he really likes me.

I dated a lot of guys and I think that was one of my downfalls. I was trying to get to know a lot of different people. I can really kick myself because I dated this one kid who was not involved in the gang. He was a really nice kid. But of course the other kids gave me a very hard time. Since it was more important to be accepted by them, I broke up with him.

All the kids in the gang had cars. And we did all kinds of dumb things, like high-speed car chases. Or we'd try to run each other off the road. We were always doing crazy things like that.

One time Robby had stolen my friend Michael's car, and Mike called the police. Robby was arrested, but he got out on bail. The next day, Mike dropped the charges against Robby. But Robby didn't know the charges were dropped and he decided to come after Michael.

A few days later Robby and his friend John saw some of us driving in Michael's car. They started chasing us down Route 6 in John's pickup truck. We were going, like, 140 miles an hour down Route 6! We had an old police car, so it handled very well.

I don't know how long they were chasing us. But it felt like a very long time. At the end we turned—hardly stepping on the brakes at all—onto Airport Road. It was pitch black, and we ran into a ditch. Thank goodness they didn't follow us there. But I'll tell you, it was one of the scariest times in my whole life.

Lots of times my parents didn't want me to go out. They would ground me. But my room was on the second floor. And while they thought that I was in my room I would climb out my window and jump down the back porch. You know, I would leave.

They really had no control over me. They didn't know what to do anymore. Everything they said went in one ear and out the other. I wasn't listening. I was always skipping school. I was always in trouble.

I think I was just starting high school then. Maybe ninth grade. God, I don't even know what year it was! Anyhow, my parents put this PINS [Person In Need of Supervision] petition on me. The school also put a PINS petition on me.

My parents and I went to Family Court. The court placed me in a group home where there were five other girls. We lived three to a room in the two upstairs rooms. There were four boys living downstairs.

I was there part of the summer between ninth and tenth grades. I made a lot of close friends while I was there. We were all kids that had gotten into trouble, even though we came from different backgrounds.

When I went there I felt, like, really isolated. I'd never ever hung out with city kids. I heard that these kids were very tough. So, of course, I went in there thinking that I would have to be tough. That way nobody would bother me.

I didn't get along with anybody for a couple of days. I forget how it started, but I got into a conversation with Barbara. They nicknamed her the "Butch Kid." She was a short girl. And she was very, very strong. She almost looked like a body builder.

Apparently she said something nasty to me. I got nasty right back. Everybody in the room just froze. It was so quiet. Nobody knew how it would come out.

Barbara and I moved in real close to start slugging it out. But then we looked into each other's face. And that was it. In a minute, I started laughing. And she started laughing, too. Then we started talking.

I said, "Why didn't you guys talk to me?"

And she said, "We thought you were a slut and stuff."

I think she said that because I walked in there wearing my ripped off sweatshirt with the Playboy logo on it. What they didn't know was that it was all I had to wear.

So I said, "No, no thank you. I'm not a slut. We don't have any of them out there where I live."

Then she asked me about myself and stuff. And we started being friends.

Barbara and I became very close. One Monday night was the breakthrough for our friendship. We made leather bracelets that night with our names on them. I made one for Barbara, and she made one for me. It was something very special. To this day I still have the bracelet she gave me.

My counselor at the group home was named Jerry. He was nice, and he helped us try to work things out. But I didn't want to stay there. So, I asked myself, "How can I get out of this?"

I quickly figured out how to work the system, so to speak. Of course, I agreed to every rule that they laid down. And they let me go home.

When I got home, my parents said, "You'll have to stay home more and not go running around."

I said to them, "The hell with you. I'm out of here."

So that first day I went to town and got high.

My parents called the Family Court back again, and they placed me in a foster home. I stayed there until the end of the summer.

The foster family knew that I loved riding. So they took me to a farm where they had horses and I rode there. And they took me to the mountains where I went rowing on a lake.

This family really did a lot with the kids.

*At the foster home, Meg gets
a chance to ride horses again.*

They made you feel very comfortable so you're real open about everything. And I think that's good. They respected us. Whatever you said didn't go back to the courts and stuff. To this day I still talk to them. I go up and see them all the time.

The foster home pretty much ran for the rest of the summer. It didn't interfere with school. I think I might have missed two days of school when I came back home.

But when I got back, I got the shock of my life. Mr. Fletcher, the vice principal, told me to sign myself out. He said, "Just sign yourself out. You'll never graduate."

I thought to myself, "Who are you to tell me that I'll never graduate? I'm a lot smarter than you ever were." That had been my attitude toward the teachers and the principals, too.

So I stayed in school. But I would always skip. I spent more days walking around than I spent going to class. I'd be cutting my classes and hiding out in the bathroom smoking cigarettes. I'd do that instead of going to class—especially if I had a test or something.

The teachers all gave me a hard time. But there were two teachers who were great. They really, really saved me. One was Mrs. Thomas, an English teacher. She wasn't my teacher, but she'd chase me around the hall with a broom whenever I'd skip. Anyhow, she saw to it that I passed English and got credit, even when I was being my most obnoxious.

What happened was this: The first or second week of my English class I got into a fight with Mr. Korn, my English teacher. He was giving me a real hard time and I got up and I used a curse word. Then I said, "Who are you to criticize me and to give us personality evaluations? Your job is to teach."

I was fresh to him because I didn't care. Even when I was younger, you didn't mess with me.

So anyhow, Mr. Korn threw me out of class and told me to go to the office—which, of course, I never did. So, for the rest of the quarter I didn't go to class.

But that's when Mrs. Thomas saved me. She realized that I didn't have English. So she offered to tutor me. She stayed with me after school and lunch hours and every time that she could. And she made me read everything. Then she got Mr. Korn to write up a test. I got a ninety-three or ninety-four on it. And I got credit for the year.

The other teacher that helped a lot was Mrs. Hope. She was my science teacher. Back in those days, I really didn't listen. So I was having a lot of trouble with the fundamentals of science, like the table of elements and so on. Mrs. Hope would always spend a lot of time helping me.

Then, one time, Mrs. Hope helped in another way. I got into a big fight with my parents. It was wintertime. I ran out of the house and was standing in front of the A & P when Mrs. Hope came by. She asked me what I was doing. I said, "Nothing."

"Well, if you're not doing anything why don't you come to my house and get warm. You look chilled to the bone."

So I went over to her house and had some soup. Then she made up a bed for me and let me sleep over. The next day when I woke up she made me go to school.

And it was right then that my whole attitude changed. Even though I still skipped every once in a while, I made up my mind to graduate.

Basically, I've always thought of school as a challenge. Even when I was having the worst trouble, I always thought education was important. So now, I tried really hard. I applied myself to school. And I ended up passing everything, though concentrating was still really hard for me.

Summer came, and I wasn't that bad. But nobody spotted my new attitude. To them, I still hung out with the same kids. And they thought I was still getting high and stuff like that. My parents found it hard to deal with that. They didn't understand that I was starting to change.

That fall I went into the tenth grade. I really wanted to sock it to my parents and teachers. So I decided to go to high school during the day and to college at night. I went to college because I wanted to show the school that they were wrong. I also wanted to keep myself busy. I knew that if I was hanging around I would eventually start getting high again.

I asked Mom if I could go. She said, "If you think you can do it. But if it's too much, you're going to have to withdraw." That was the agreement.

So I signed up. Here I was, fourteen years old, going to college. I took psychology and sociology as my first two courses. God only knows why!

But I pulled C's in both of them. I'm amazed now to think that I even passed at that age.

At first, though, I was a little discouraged. But my parents said, "C is good. I got C's when I was in college."

After tenth grade, I had enough courses so I skipped eleventh, and I went right into twelfth grade. I was doing well.

The year that I moved to twelfth I was feeling physically better. I could get back into things. In fact, it was then that I got back into gymnastics. That was good. I made the team.

So now I was hanging out with all the old friends that I did gymnastics with in grade school. That was a weird scene. Two of these friends, Jean and Laurie, had been very close to me. We did Girl Scouts together and stuff like that.

Jean and I were very competitive. We were the ones who did back handsprings and that stuff in grade school. Laurie had not really developed her gymnastic skills as much. Really, I was much stronger and better than them in grade school.

Now, though, Jean and Laurie were like the two stars of the team. So it was, like, "Wow! If you had just stuck with it can you imagine what you could be doing now, Meg girl?"

At first, when I made the team, we didn't really say much to each other. Then one day I just went up to them and I said, "Hi." And soon we were talking.

After a while, Laurie said, "Oh, Meg, we thought you didn't like us any more."

And I said, "Funny, that was just the impression I got."

And they said, "Oh no, no."

"Well," I said, "I made a lot of rotten remarks to you over the last few years. I take it all back."

They were real nice. They said, "Don't worry about it."

The first time I got up on the floor for a

gymnastics meet was at our high school. It wasn't a real meet. It was just a practice.

But was I shaking! You could probably see me shaking from a mile away. I was so nervous. I started out with this dance routine. I was never graceful, never. I did tumbling best. I was good at that. But I was never graceful for the dance routines.

I probably looked okay, but I didn't feel very good. Everybody was rooting me on, though. I heard them shouting, "Go on, Meg. Go for it!"

I think I scored a six, which wasn't bad. They don't give you nine or ten in high school. Then it was, like, "Hey! This is fun." That was another turning point in my life.

Because I went to college at night, I couldn't go to all the meets. My school came before the meets and that was that. Besides, they knew that if I had a college class I couldn't go.

I applied myself a lot during that year. I looked at my classes and I saw I was doing high school and college at the same time. That made me feel very proud.

That next year in college I took statistics at night and I pulled an A in it. I don't remember the other courses I took. At any rate, I did well. I think I pulled a B in every other class. And it was a lot of fun.

During the day, when I needed to relax, I

Meg graduates high school.

would go out to the smoking section near the high school gym. I would come out there with my stack of books and sit down, light up a cigarette, and talk with the kids that hung around there.

This was the spot where everybody got high and stuff like that. I didn't really hang out with the kids from grade school. Number one, I didn't think they would accept me. Number two, I was too busy to even bother with them.

It meant a lot to me to be able to walk out behind the gym and think, "Hey, you can do well in school and still hang out."

It was sort of like a challenge. Like, "Let's see how they react to this. Will they still accept me or what will they do?"

I wanted to prove myself to the school. I didn't want my parents to be hurt any more. My father lost a lot of business when I got into trouble. That's because everyone knows what's happening in a small town. And I just didn't want my parents to be disappointed in me any more. That was important. I was old enough to realize that it mattered.

Things kept going well my last year in high school. I did the gymnastics. And I did everything else that I wanted to do. And then boom, I was graduated!

I was only sixteen when I got out of school. Right away I started dating this guy, Steve. My sister was dating a guy named Mike. Steve was Mike's best friend.

It turned out that Steve was heavily involved with cocaine. He dealt cocaine. And that summer I really fell on my face from cocaine.

As a matter of fact, we all got arrested for dealing cocaine. My sister, too. The four of us. Everybody read about it in the newspaper.

To make things worse, I was living with Steve at the time. And I got pregnant.

That was really scary. For some reason, Mike and Steve weren't getting along at the time. And because something happened between the guys, Ellen and I weren't getting along. So I couldn't even talk to her about it.

One night, about two months after I got pregnant, Steve was really wired. We got into a fist fight. He punched me around. I was in a lot of pain. It was awful. Then, a few days later, Steve was sentenced to jail for dealing cocaine.

After Steve left, I moved back home. I was crying one night because my stomach hurt so bad. So I went and told my Mom about the pregnancy. She took me and I had an abortion.

It was very hard. But it was for the best as far as I was concerned.

While Steve was in jail, I drove an hour every day to go see him, and an hour home. But I knew that after he got out of jail everything would be

Meg, picked up by the police for cocaine dealing, is fingerprinted.

different. I didn't want to be dating or living with him any more.

When he asked about the baby, I told him a lie. I said that I had lost it. I knew that he wanted to have the baby. And I just didn't want to get involved in that, especially with him in jail.

Steve got out of jail that summer. One night we were out driving on this dark road. I was behind the wheel. He was all wasted. That's when I told him I didn't want to date him any more. So he pulls this knife on me in the car. He really scared me. We were alone on this dark road, and I was screaming my head off.

I yelled at him, "Get out of the car." But he wouldn't go. So I tried to get out of the car. He just pulled me back in.

I must say that I totally freaked out. I said, "You son of a bitch. You just cut me! Get out of this car."

I can't remember exactly what else I said to him—it was all so frightening. The reason was that he wasn't really all there because of the coke.

Then he lifted the knife up high. I was sure that was the end. But then, instead of cutting me, he started cutting his own arm.

So I screamed again, "Get out of the car."

At that moment I was able to open the door and jump out of the car. But he got out, too. I yelled at him, "Don't come near me with that knife!"

So he threw the knife away. Then he said, "You're really weird. Get back in the car. Drive me back to town."

He got in, and I drove to the movie theater where my sister worked as a cashier. Inside the theater, I got on the phone without Steve knowing it. I called my father and I told him what happened. He said he'd be right over.

Then Steve came toward me. He said, "Let's talk. Let's just go somewhere and talk."

I said, "No, I got to go." He must have realized something was up because he left.

In a few minutes, my dad pulled up. He got out of the car and ran over to me. He said, "Are you okay?"

I just said, "Yeah."

And he said, "I just wanted to make sure." He looked so scared I almost started to cry.

Then I got in my car and headed home. Dad followed me in his car. He wanted to make sure I was okay and that Steve didn't come after me or anything like that.

In the summer of 1988 I was seventeen years old. I got a good job. It was for an architect, a friend of my father's. I still had a bad problem, though, snorting cocaine. And I was dealing a little bit, too. But I needed even more money for my habit.

So I started taking money from the guy I was working for. I was the secretary in the office. Half the time I was the only one there. My boss was hardly ever in the office. Sometimes we had a couple of guys that did drafting work that came in. But that was about it.

What I did was write checks bigger than they should be. Say we had a bill for $300. I would write a check to myself for $500. And then I'd pay the $300 bill myself. I'd keep the extra $200.

I was working for him about a year or so before he found out what I was doing. I had taken a lot of money by then. But I owed a lot of money to the guys I was dealing drugs with. They always gave me a lot of credit. And, of course, the more I had on credit, the more drugs I did. It was just like a credit card. The more you have, the more you spend.

In the meantime, I was dating a new guy. And I had bought a nice new sports car for myself. It's sitting in my parents' yard now. My new boyfriend looked a lot like Steve. I guess that was part of the reason I went out with him.

One day we were driving down to the Mobil station to get gas. Steve and his friend were sitting there in a pickup truck. I think they were high.

When they saw me, Steve's friend came over and started getting really nasty. "I hear you said this and this about me," he said.

So I got out of the car and started shooting my mouth off. I got a big mouth, you know. I said, "Get lost. I never said anything about you."

He said, "Shut up, or I'll come over and slap you."

And I said, "Yeah, right. Come on over and try."

After three or four minutes of me antagonizing him to do it, he hit me. And when he did, I kicked him square in the groin. I punched him in the face a couple of times, too. We had it out right there, in front of the Mobil station.

The guy I was with was out of the car, too. But he wasn't much good. He was weak. I'm much stronger than he is.

Before long, I had Steve's friend on the ground. That's when Steve came out of the truck. He jumped on me from behind.

So Steve and I had it out. I swung out at him. I had nails at the time, and when I swung at him, I cut him real bad. I got him right across the face. And then I punched him so hard that his eye started to bleed. I can remember this vividly. After that, I left.

I didn't know this, but a guy getting gas at Mobil was a friend of my father's. He called the police. By the time they came, I had left. But the police found me. And I told them what happened.

Then the police went out and picked up Steve and his friend. And basically, they ran the two of them out of town. They told them never to come back.

That was really the last time I saw Steve. I kept dating other guys but I was still on drugs at the time. A few months later, in August, I got fired from my job because of the money I took. It came to around $18,000. But I wasn't arrested at that time.

My boss said, like, "I want it all at once or not at all." He wanted my parents to take out a loan to pay him back all the money. But they wouldn't do it. Finally, he agreed to let me pay him back a little at a time.

Anyhow, things were really messed up. And that's when it finally hit me.

"Meg," I said to myself, "you had better get some help before it's too late."

I knew about a two-year program run by the Mental Health Department or something. But I really didn't want to go into that. I think I would have resented being there. I just wasn't too keen on being away for two whole years.

I kept thinking about it, though. Then, about two weeks later, my Mom confronted me. "How do you feel about going away to a thirty-day rehab program?'' she said.

I was a little surprised. ''Well, it's not the nicest thing in the world,'' I said. ''But I really think I need it.''

Until then, I thought that no one had any idea that I was an addict. I thought I really knew how to hide it, that I hid it from everybody. I really didn't think my parents knew. I had told them that after Steve I went clean. But somehow, my Mom knew it. And, of course, inside, I knew I was hooked.

So I spoke with Eva Stein. She was head of Human Resources in town. She got me a sponsor and someone to pay for me to go to rehab in Pennsylvania.

The next thing I know, the people in Pennsylvania called me. They asked all kinds of questions. ''What drugs were you doing? How long have you been doing them? What's your age? How did you do in school? How do you get along with your family? Do you have a boyfriend?'' And everything like that.

This was on a Friday night, September 22. That day was mine, my mother's, and my best friend Annie's birthdays. We all have the same birthday! So they said, ''Well, do you want to come now or leave in the morning?''

''I'll come in the morning,'' I told them.

So anyway, the next day, my parents drove me down to Pennsylvania. It was really weird when I got there. I didn't know what to expect. It was very beautiful. The leaves were just beginning to change color.

After my parents left, I was walking around the main building. And all of a sudden, I heard a voice that sounded familiar. I turned around and heard someone say, "Hey, Meg, how are you?"

It was my friend Peter's father! He was an alcoholic. We had always known this about him. And here he was. Seeing someone from back home sort of made me feel better.

Being in rehab was a new thing for me. The first week I thought I'd go out of my mind. Because, of course, it was cold turkey. I had been doing cocaine up until then and now I had none. I had terrible shakes. I also had really weird dreams or hallucinations. It was like when you're half awake and half asleep—only much worse.

And I couldn't sleep. I would pace around all night. I'd walk around with the counselors because I just couldn't sleep.

This was happening as I went through withdrawal. But then everything pretty much settled down. That's what's important.

In rehab, you get up in the morning and all day long you go to groups. We had one group in the afternoon that was role-playing. There was this big black guy named Bill in the group. In the end he became a real teddy bear, and he and I became best friends.

In the beginning, Bill always intimidated me. I hated him and gave him a hard time, like saying to him, "You ain't nothing. You're nothing but a junkie. And you'll be a junkie for the rest of your life." It took a long time before we got along.

Anyway, Bill and Lamar, another guy in the group, were having this role-playing. Lamar was playing himself. And Bill was playing Lamar's girlfriend. As they were talking it turned out that Lamar's girlfriend had lost a baby. She had an abortion.

That was it. I just broke down and started crying my eyes out. That got the counselor talking. "Let's bring that out, Meg. What's bothering you? What's wrong? Tell us about it, Meg."

So I tried to bring it all out. But it was really, really hard. I had never actually talked about it. I think the hardest thing—though maybe it was just an excuse—was that Peter's father was there. I started going through the whole thing. But they could tell I was holding back.

Then someone said, "That's baloney! You're not really opening up. There's something more going on."

So, I brought it all out. I told things I never thought I'd ever tell anybody. It all came out. And I must say, it felt better when I got through.

The thing I brought up that hurt the most was about Steve. I told how he was always very physically abusive to me. Yet I was always sticking up for him.

I remember one time when we were living in Chatham. He started beating me up behind the garage. It was maybe the second day we were there. He was throwing me up against the wall and things like that. Just at that moment some of Steve's friends drove by. They said, "Hey, Steve, stop that! Leave her alone." But then they drove away. And he just kept on punching me and throwing me around.

Until rehab, though, I had totally forgotten about that incident. In fact, I always told people that Steve and I got along pretty well. I had never talked to anyone about the beatings.

There was so much I had forgotten. I just couldn't absorb all the things that were happening to me. I don't know what it was.

Being in rehab was almost like playing a mind game. They made you dig down into your brain. It was intense, very intense, treatment.

One of the groups was run by, well, we called him Mr. Addiction. His real name was Aaron. He was a black man. Like all the counselors, he

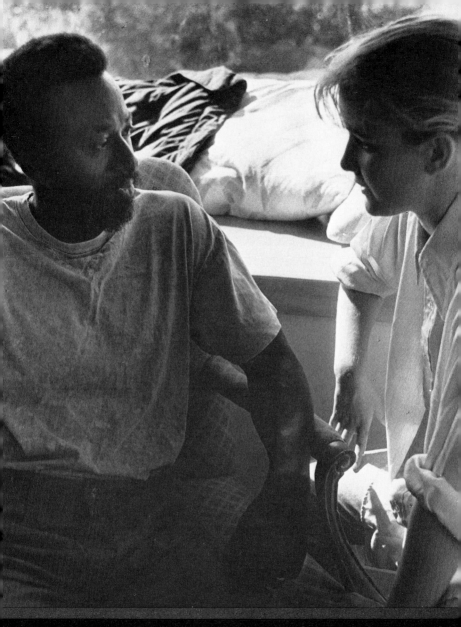

*Aaron and Meg talk together
at the rehab center.*

had been addicted. But he had been off drugs for many years.

Aaron was good. He knew what he was doing. He made even the best of the group break down in tears by the time he was done.

The day before you left, that's when Aaron really made you face your addictions. He'd say, like, "Yeah, yeah, I'm Mr. Addiction, and I'll be waiting for you down at the end of the drive-way."

And you'd say, "C'mon, Aaron, you know I'll be good."

Then he'd say, "What about the time when you were fourteen . . ." You know, he'd bring out personal things that he knew about. These were things that were in the file. "What about when your father came into the room and you were beating on your Mom?" Or, "What about the time you stole to pay for your habit?"

Aaron would just go on and on and on. And you'd have to be very careful with what you said. If you took too long to answer, he'd say, "C'mon, what's the matter? Ain't you got nothing to say?" You really had to bounce right back at him.

One time Aaron really nailed me. He said, "C'mon, Miss Goody Two Shoes, Straight-A student. You know those days are all over."

And I said, "They're not over. I'm going back to school."

But he went on. "Look, your school days are over. You're never going back. And forget about your family. You're not going to be seeing them any more, either. You're going to be heading right back to your friend Steve. You can't stay away from him. And as soon as you do, you'll meet me waiting for you at the corner."

I said, "Oh, no, you won't catch me."

And he said, "Oh, yeah, don't you worry. I'll be waiting. I'll always be waiting for you."

A lot of the counseling at the rehab is clarifying specific situations. You learn when you have to really keep your guard up. You come to understand the attitude behind what you do. You begin to ask questions: "What would you do if this happened? What would you think? Would your attitude have to change?"

I never really realized until I went through the rehab program that I had a fear of men. It wasn't an enormous fear, but still I was afraid of men. I think it came from what I had been through—because of Steve. And because of something that happened before that.

It was back in eighth grade. I was with this guy and he raped me.

I know I didn't mention it before. It's hard to talk about it.

I was already sexually active. And I was always flirting. But I was very naive. I was dating this guy, and we went out one night. We were hanging out in the back of the school. We were in this dark corner making out when he said, "Let's do it."

I said, "No! I don't want to."

And he said, "Oh, yes you do!"

So he pushed me down and held me there. I tried to get up, but I couldn't. He was too strong. And he raped me.

Afterwards, I just got my bag and left. I ran home and I cried for a while. But I didn't want to talk about it. I just couldn't bring it out.

Now I know that this definitely changed the way I felt about men. Up until then I had, like, a fairytale idea about men. I thought that they would fall in love with me. From then on, I really didn't expect anything from them.

And for a long while after it seemed that you had sex and that was that. That was the way it was done. It just wasn't as important as before. It didn't even mean anything to me. My attitude was, "Let's just get it over with."

On October 20 I got out of rehab. At first it was tough. When I got out of the rehab my parents wanted me to go stay in a halfway house. But I didn't want to. So we had a fight and didn't speak to each other for a long time. It took about four months before we really started talking again.

That's when I went to live with Michael.

Michael was my boyfriend from before the rehab. I knew he was going to be waiting for me when I got out. We spoke on the phone sometimes when I was in Pennsylvania.

So Michael and I moved into a little apartment. I got a job at White's Drug Store. He was working for a roofer. But two of the guys who were working with him used to get stoned every day. So Michael quit that job. He didn't want me to be upset by the whole thing. "I don't want them to come around the house," he said.

Michael and I are still together. We have a really good relationship. It's going on two years. And we both can't believe it. Like, "Oh, my God! Don't say anything. Don't say anything that might ruin it."

Of course, we have our share of grievances against each other. It's very hard at this particular time. Business is very slow. He does odd jobs and he can't always find work. I think the biggest arguments we have are financial. We really don't have any other conflicts.

Michael has always been very supportive of me. He took me to AA [Alcoholics Anonymous]. He even went to a few AA meetings with me. But then I said, "No, that's not a good program for me. I have to look for another program."

That's when I joined PRIDE, a place where they help kids get off drugs. I've been going there

*Meg, living with Michael, finds him supportive
and caring. She is finally beating her addiction.*

now for well over a year. I think AA and NA [Narcotics Anonymous] were okay, but I didn't really get enough out of them. It just seemed to me it was like hearing the same old story all over again. It was more depressing than helpful sometimes.

Thanks to the rehab and PRIDE, I'm finally beginning to understand myself a little better. There are still some parts of my personality that aren't the greatest. But I'm trying to learn how to handle them.

I'm sure I have an addictive personality because of genes and heredity. I watched my grandfather die of alcoholism. So I was always very apprehensive of drinking and veered away from alcohol. But I did get into drugs. I showed my addictive behavior that way.

In fact, my addictive personality influences everything—and I do mean everything—that I do. When I become addicted to my schoolwork, I forget about everything else. If I'm not careful, I do everything to excess. And that includes eating. There are some days when I have the poorest eating habits. I'm not hungry, so I just pick up a box of chocolates and eat them the whole day. That's something I really have to work on.

They worked on my eating habits at PRIDE. That was a big thing. I'd have to make lists of what I ate the whole week. When I'd look at it,

I thought to myself, "That's pretty disgusting what you're putting into your body." And we'd work on it—eating salads and eating vegetables.

My cholesterol is 280, and I've had chest pains. I must confess that my biggest, biggest treat is a double hero with roast beef and melted cheese! I'd go to hell for one of those! But getting to say no to it—that's another challenge.

My temper is something else I have to deal with. It's not gone. It'll never be gone. But I'm getting a lot better at handling it.

Just the other day I got into an argument with Michael's father. He was blaming me for something my sister had done. I was getting real upset. A few years ago, I probably would have called him a dirty name. Or maybe I would have even punched him out. But now I said, "Be quiet! I don't want to hear it." And then I turned around and walked away from him.

I had another whole personality change after the rehab. Before, I took a lot. Whatever you threw on me, I took. Like, "That's fine. Go ahead. Do whatever you want."

You could walk all over me and I wouldn't care. Oh sure, I always was tough. But when it came to relationships, I always got the bad end of the deal.

At rehab they said I didn't take care of myself as much as I should. I didn't give myself enough credit. I didn't respect myself enough to say, "No, I'm not going to take beatings and other stuff any more."

The counselors at rehab said, "Don't take it." They told me this after I told them one story of what happened in my relationship with my old boyfriend, Steve.

Steve and I got engaged just before he went into jail. He bought me a nice diamond ring.

Then, two weeks after he went to jail, I found out that he had put it on *my* credit card! That meant I had to pay for the ring he gave me! In other words, he left me with this enormous bill. Being the idiot I was, I paid it.

Every time I'd tell them stuff like that, the counselors would say, "Don't take it. You're too good a person. You've got a lot of potential. You've got a big mouth, so use it! Start looking out for number one. You have to take care of yourself before you can take care of anybody else."

The whole thing is, you've got to start loving yourself before you can love anybody else. In the past, I really didn't. I didn't take care of myself. Even when I talked about myself, I'd be very negative.

It's been a long road back for me. Now I go to PRIDE every week. Being in a group, you see kids come in who are on their first week of staying clean. And you can see the attitude that I had

*The **PRIDE** meetings have proven especially helpful to Meg.*

my second or third week in rehab. It was, like, "Yeah, yeah, yeah—I know everything."

So you call them on it. "C'mon, let's cut the baloney. C'mon, you know you're lying." Or I say, "You're full of it. Don't you think that your life is a little more important than that?"

Then you see either a look of shock or they say, "Yeah, I guess you're right." Just to see or hear that makes me feel really good.

Different kids keep going in and out of our group. One kid that was in there ended up stabbing somebody. So he didn't make it. But there are three of us in the group that have been there a long time, and we have all become pretty good friends.

We find that when one of us slips back into a baloney routine, we get called on it. And I think that's important. It's like a real family.

Everything's anonymous. Same way as AA. I think it was easier for me because the kids in PRIDE are my own age. The people in NA were a lot older than that. Some were kids that I used to get high with. I couldn't express everything that I wanted to with them around. I just didn't feel comfortable.

One of the kids at PRIDE is still in high school. He's a nice kid. He's just typical. Not one of the bad kids, like I was.

PRIDE works like this: We have group sessions. If we don't have something that we want to bring up on our own, they'll bring out a tape to show us or mention something they want to discuss. There's always an interchange between the counselor and the rest of us, which I think is good.

I go once a week for individual therapy. But in addition, there's always an open-door policy. So if something happens, you just go in or you pick up the phone and find someone to talk to.

So now, I'm back in college. But it wasn't easy. I wanted to go back right after rehab, but I couldn't afford it. So I went in with all my tax papers and everything and they told me I had earned too much money that year to get financial aid.

That really hurt. Here, for the first time, I was trying to do something good for myself, and the college tells me I can't do it! So I told them everything I'd been through. I got all the court information from my lawyer and everything and sent it to the college.

The people at the college checked and verified the amounts and everything. Then they finally accepted me and put me on a special scholarship. The woman said, ''People trying to do better deserve a break.''

I started school on my birthday. I have to admit that it was the best birthday I'd had in years.

I took accounting, calculus, literature, and speech class. I got an A in everything, but a B in calculus.

At the end of the term, I went to the post office twice a day waiting for my grades to come in. About the sixth time I went in, there it was. I'll tell you, I nearly passed out.

So I pulled out the envelope and opened it r-e-a-l slowly. Then, "WHEEEEE! Look at that!"

Around eight people looked at me like I was absolutely stone crazy. Some of the people knew me. They were asking, "Well, how did you do?" and stuff like that. And when I took it home, my parents were really proud.

It's really amazing that I'm back to this point. When I got to college, I really applied myself. At first, Michael got frustrated with me because when I was at home I always had a book in my face. So he goes, "C'mon, c'mon, let's go to bed or something."

But I said, "No, I have to study."

After a while Michael stopped bugging me about studying. He realized that it was that important to me. But it was hard for him. Even though he was always good in school, he was never an A student.

Now I'm devoting most of my time to school. I also do house cleaning. It keeps me busy and pays the bills. My family and I have a very good relationship now. I'm horseback riding again and I hope to show this spring.

I went up to my old high school the other day and told the principal how I did. He just stood there and said, "Oh, my God, I can't believe it. That's fantastic."

Then he told everyone who was in the office. He even told Mrs. Kay, who was the one that would always send me down to the office. And she said, "Never underestimate anybody. If I ever get frustrated, especially with a kid who's having problems, I'll think of you and say that he or she could make it one of these days." That made me feel very good.

I've been completely off drugs for about two years. To be honest, I still do miss them sometimes. But all I have to do is look at what my life was like three years ago and that's enough of a deterrent. I always say, if my life isn't enough of a deterrent to drugs, I don't know what is!

In all seriousness, it's true. If I had lived my life without drugs, I can imagine where I'd be at now. Maybe I'd have a master's degree in finance!

But I'm still not going to let that get me down. And I'm not going to knock my parents at all. I think they did the best they could. I don't think I can criticize them in any way. I think what happened was that I couldn't handle it. It wasn't their fault that I got involved with drugs. It wasn't their fault that I just fell apart. I think my mother feels guilty, even though she says she doesn't.

The message for parents is, "Don't blame yourself." I think that it's important for parents—not only the children—to have counseling. And parents need to know that it's not just the kids that are doing poorly in school that get into trouble. It's also kids like me.

I know my parents had a lot of guilt for sending me away to rehab, but it was probably the best thing that could have happened. I didn't agree with them at first. But I did come to believe that they shouldn't have felt guilty about that. They shouldn't feel that it's their fault. They shouldn't say, "If I had done this or that, things would have worked out differently."

In a lot of ways I'm thankful that I went through the drugs after the accident. If I went through the drugs later or when I wasn't under my parents' care, I'd be in a whole lot more trouble. I don't know if I would have ever made it without everybody's support and everybody being there. I mean, I give all the credit in the world to my parents for putting up with me.

This last year has really been a whole new, fresh start. And it's really proving something to me, too. Like I can still do it. I think in a way maybe it's also proving something to other people. Not so much the friends I used to hang out with in grade school. They know what I was like. But their parents or anybody else who doesn't know me—except for what they read in the paper about me getting into trouble.

What it all boils down to is that everything I've done is really for myself. I have a saying, "In the end, the only one you can count on is yourself. Don't try to impress anybody else, because that's not going to impress you."

One thing everybody says—my counselors and all. "Don't ever think it's easy."

That's the best advice you can get. Because as soon as you think it's easy, you have the attitude that if you do drugs once it's not going to matter. But then, if you do it once, you feel guilty. And if you do it again, you feel real bad because you're ruining your whole program and all your years of being drug free.

It's always going to be hard for me. But that doesn't mean that I always have to drone on about it. I know I can never let my guard down. I must always be aware of my addictions. Whenever I'm confronted with a party situation—which happens a lot to me—what do I do? Do I pick up the drink or don't pick up the drink? Smoke a joint or don't smoke a joint? That's something I'll have to deal with forever. But if I do deal with it, I'm sure that things will work out okay.

For More Information/ Hotline Numbers

Al-Anon and Alateen
200 Park Avenue
New York, NY 10016
1-212-254-7230
Hotline: 1-800-252-6465

Alcoholics Anonymous (AA)
P.O. Box 459
Grand Central Station
New York, NY 10017
1-212-473-6200
Hotline: Look in local Yellow Pages under "Alcoholism"

Alcohol and Drug Referral Hotline
1-800-252-6465

American Council for Drug Education
5820 Hubbard Drive
Rockville, MD 20852
1-301-294-0600

American Council on Marijuana and Other
Psychoactive Drugs (ACM)
6193 Executive Blvd.
Rockville, MD 20852
1-301-294-0600

Drug Enforcement Administration (DEA)
Office of Public Affairs
1405 I Street, NW
Washington, DC 20012
1-202-633-1000

Narcotics Anonymous (NA)
(Look in local White Pages under "Narcotics Anonymous")

National Cocaine Hotline
1-800-262-2463

National Council on Child Abuse and Family Violence
1-800-222-2000

National Council on Alcoholism
1-800-NCA-CALL

National Institute of Drug Abuse, Drug Information,
and Treatment
1-800-662-4357

National Runaway Switchboard and Suicide Hotline
1-800-621-4000

PRIDE (Parent Resource Institute and Drug Education)
Drug Information Hotline
1-800-677-7433